TCHOTCHKES

AND THEIR

F*CKED-UP
THOUGHTS

WHIMSICAL

With more personality than purpose, these tchotchkes might look fun and frivolous, but be forewarned, looks can be deceiving. Beneath their playful exteriors lies an untapped world of sass and sarcasm.

Hula Girl

Keep your toxic masculinity
away from my coconuts!
How about you try endlessly
hula-ing in a Barbie body
with impossible proportions
and an itchy grass skirt?
I might be an object but
I refuse to be objectified.

🝔 **CARE AND HANDLING**
Hands-off, knuckle-dragger!

📍 **IDEAL LOCATION IN HOME**
Anywhere but barefoot in your kitchen.

VIRGO

Opening the fridge again, huh?
No judgment here. Of course
not. Nope, this is a judgment-
free zone. Oh, ok, just gonna dip
that finger right into the ranch,
huh? No shame here. This is a
safe space. Gonna eat those little
weenies right out of packet then?
You go, girl. You do you.
Like I said, no judgment here.

💧 **CARE AND HANDLING**
Easy on the door! I'm barely hanging on.

📍 **IDEAL LOCATION IN HOME**
I thought that "fridge" part was obvious.

TAURUS

Plastic Fruit
Fridge Magnet

Wind-Up Toy

I'm all wound up. I see
Nurse Barbie next week.
I expect a diagnosis of PTSD.
Yes, just like G.I. Joe.
Shell shock. I was never
in combat with Cobra
Commander, but I spent a
week in a dental office treasure
box with glow-in-the-dark
snakes and clown stickers.

🌢 **CARE AND HANDLING**
None. No care. No handling.

📍 **IDEAL LOCATION IN HOME**
Anywhere but the toy box.

SCORPIO

Creepy? Little ol' me? I'm just as sweet as pie and would never tiptoe around in tiny porcelain shoes to breathe ancient curses into your ears as you sleep. Goodness no!

◊ **CARE AND HANDLING**
Keep me close and never leave me.

📍 **IDEAL LOCATION IN HOME**
Bedroom shelf, where I can gaze at you endlessly with my big, childlike eyes. Sweet dreams!

PISCES

Ceramic Hummel Figurine

Lava Lamp

I said "nightlife," not "night-light!" Nothing about my rock 'n' roll lifestyle prepared me to become a bauble for a hipster. What kind of ambience am I creating here? Where are the hookers and white drugs?!

💧 **CARE AND HANDLING**
Play some Pink Floyd or turn down the volume. That's not lava; it's my ears bleeding from your Indie Folk.

📍 **IDEAL LOCATION IN HOME**
Is there a medicine cabinet? I need a fix.

LEO

Oh, so you think I'm waving hello? I'm waving goodbye, you graceless buffoon! Get your pestilent aura out of my blessed space. If only my cute little paws had claws.

💧 **CARE AND HANDLING**
Touch me again, and I'll put another "ow" in "meow."

📍 **IDEAL LOCATION IN HOME**
Place me in a patch of sunlight on a high shelf. I can nap, and you can move out immediately.

GEMINI

Lucky Cat

MANEKI-NEKO

Snow Globe

Dreaming of a white Christmas? I am, too. Ship me back to Vienna where I belong! Play all the Bing Crosby you want, but the only thing white about Christmas in this subtropical strip mall is the cocaine smuggled in.

🝫 **CARE AND HANDLING**

Holy shit, be gentle, I'm not a cocktail—though I know you need a few to get through the day around here. I could use one, too. Replace my water with gin, and we'll be in business.

📍 **IDEAL LOCATION IN HOME**

Sure, put me next to the pink flamingo and the weird palm tree.

LEO

Quantum entanglement shows that neutrinos affect each other instantly across space time, I say, and all that comes out is "SQUAAAWKK!" Leveraging Heisenberg's principles of uncertainty and wave-particle duality, we could transcend classical information theory. "SQUAAAWKK." Dammit! Not that humans would understand anyway. These clowns designed my vocal cords.

🌢 **CARE AND HANDLING**
Can I at least have some rubber pants?

📍 **IDEAL LOCATION IN HOME**
What does it matter? I give up.

AQUARIUS

Rubber Chicken

Bobblehead Doll

Yep, yep. Great idea.
You are brilliant, sir!
I absolutely support that.
You are completely right.
Couldn't be more right.
Genius, truly!

🌢 CARE AND HANDLING

Gentle, please, I'm not a maraca. Wait,
am I a maraca? I love being a maraca!

📍 IDEAL LOCATION IN HOME

Gee, I'm just a fan of the whole place!
This is a fantastic spot. I love this spot.
Oh man, it's great here.

WHATEVER YOU WANT ME TO BE!

27

VINTAGE AND COLLECTIBLES

Take a trip down memory lane with these vintage treasures and collectible gems. Each piece has a history and, very likely, a well-earned grudge or two. They've seen it all, from glory days to garage sales, and they have some thoughts they'd like to share.

These digital pip-squeaks have no idea. Back in my day, there was no "cloud" mumbo jumbo. When I was a young clock, I had to wind my own arms . . . backwards both ways . . . in a snowstorm . . . with mahogany feet, no less!

◊ CARE AND HANDLING

Careful there, whippersnapper. I've got stiff gears and an aching pendulum.

◉ IDEAL LOCATION IN HOME

Right next to that fine porcelain bust on the mantelpiece. A little closer, please. What's your name, doll?

CAPRICORN

Miniature
Grandfather Clock

Brass Sundial

Your Egyptian ancestors understood the Earth's rotation and orbit, the precise tilt of its axis, minute seasonal changes, and the sophisticated geometry of shadows. And here you are, after centuries of evolution, and I can't help you tell your ass from your elbow even when the sun is shining.

◖ **CARE AND HANDLING**
I just need sun. SUN. You know, that big, bright ball in the sky?!

◉ **IDEAL LOCATION IN HOME**
Outside. That place with the air and the shadows.

CAPRICORN

No winding. Hands off.
"Für Elise" was majestic
the first thousand times,
but even Beethoven would
beg for mercy by now.
Turn that tiny handle one more
time, and I just may play
"Free Bird," the live version
with three guitar solos.

● CARE AND HANDLING
Don't touch me. We're through.
I mean it this time.

♥ IDEAL LOCATION IN HOME
Misplace me, along with all your
hopes and dreams.

PISCES

Vintage Music Box

Antique Compass

A little stillness please, bucko. I'm aligning with Earth's magnetic field. You know, the geomagnetic poles? Yes, it's complicated, my friend. Follow my little spinny-thingy, and I just might be able to direct the dim spark of your consciousness out of the primordial ooze.

◆ **CARE AND HANDLING**
Just don't put me next to your magnet collection. Lord knows, you're confused enough already.

◉ **IDEAL LOCATION IN HOME**
A windowsill facing south. The other south! Never mind.

SAGITTARIUS

I'm up here on the shelf, looking cool, thank goodness. I know all about my less-fortunate buddies on the track in the basement, circling endlessly with you in your big-boy conductor hat chanting, "Chug, chug, toot, toot, off we go!"

◊ CARE AND HANDLING
Pull my little handle, station master.

♥ IDEAL LOCATION IN HOME
Just keep me away from small, chubby-kneed humans. They're all unhinged.

TAURUS

Vintage Model Train

Leather-Bound
Journal

No, no, your poetry is profound.
I especially love the part that
says, "My heart is so sore. Feels
slammed in a door. Beats no
more. Poor me. Poor, poor."
I'm totally listening and
deeply moved. I only appear
to be setting myself on fire.

◊ CARE AND HANDLING
Do you think if I give myself enough
papercuts I'll cease to exist?

♥ IDEAL LOCATION IN HOME
Tucked on a shelf next to the real poets.
May I suggest Sylvia Plath?

LIBRA

Thank your lucky stars I'm made of wood, pal. Otherwise, I'd have a few choice words about the time you played "house" with me and that porcelain pig.

💧 **CARE AND HANDLING**
Maybe dust me now and then? I bet Seabiscuit never looked this tragic.

📍 **IDEAL LOCATION IN HOME**
In your freaky menagerie with the three-legged poodle and beakless duck.

TAURUS

Wooden Horse

Antique Teacup and Saucer Set

Is it time for a spot of tea? Jolly good, I adore cucumber sandwiches and buttered teacakes. Gracious, what's that you say? Cold pizza and Gatorade again?! Sod off, bloody wanker! Remove me from this Yankee hovel at once, you daft arsebadger.

CARE AND HANDLING

The dishwasher?! I'd rather perish. That dodgy contraption is pure codswallop.

IDEAL LOCATION IN HOME

In the drawing room, good sir—oh wait, I mean in "that there TV room, dadgummit!" I'm still perfecting the local dialect.

LIBRA

Ah, mon amour, I dream of cobbled streets and flaky croissants, but mostly of the fountain pen's kiss. Un petit bisou. That delicate flowing cursive, ahhhh . . . the looping flourish, oh yes . . . le plunge of the period. Oui! Une cigarette, s'il vous plaît.

🩸 **CARE AND HANDLING**

Mon Dieu! Send me back to Paris immédiatement!

📍 **IDEAL LOCATION IN HOME**

Tucked gently in the corner of a mirror. I'm a fragile whisper from the past, not a coaster.

LIBRA

Vintage Postcard

Souvenir Spoon

Gag you with a spoon? Really?!
More like gag me with your
bacteria-riddled mouth. I'm
a souvenir, meant to hold
memories, not shuttle cream of
mushroom to your disgusting
piehole! Your fingers are
grubby, too. Don't touch me.
Don't even look at me.

🝆 **CARE AND HANDLING**
Dust occasionally with an extendable
duster. Fully extended. Try not to breathe.

📍 **IDEAL LOCATION IN HOME**
A special display rack with glass
would be nice. Thick glass.

CANCER

CULTURAL
AND
ARTISANAL

From the far corners of the world
and the depths of your local
flea market, these tchotchkes bring
a touch of cultural flair and a lot of
artisanal attitude. They might look
like they belong in a museum, but
trust us, their thoughts definitely
shouldn't be on display.

Ever wonder what it's like to be jam-packed with ever smaller versions of yourself? Yeah, just as insane as you might imagine. Big Olga picks fights with little Svetlana, and middle-sized Elena is a compulsive liar. Itsy bitsy Katya's muffled giggling haunts us all. Talk about multiple personality disorder.

💧 **CARE AND HANDLING**
Open with care. Don't vacuum up tiniest-baby-me.

📍 **IDEAL LOCATION IN HOME**
Take us apart and line us up on the shelf, please. Third-me is claustrophobic.

GEMINI

Russian Nesting Dolls

MATRYOSHKA DOLLS

Mexican Folk-Art Sculpture

ALEBRIJE

I have the head of a fire-breathing dragon, the multi-colored wings of a giant eagle, and a neon ass with the coiled tail of a serpent. You calling me a freak? Go ahead, look at me sideways. Órale, pendejo.

◗ CARE AND HANDLING
Is that Windex? ¡Ay, caramba! Sponge baths in Sacred Agua de Florida, por favor.

♥ IDEAL LOCATION IN HOME
I belong in the spirit realm, not the "art nook." I've seen your 75-inch flat screen TV. Don't tell me you can't afford a spirit realm.

SCORPIO

Hey, man, do you ever just hang out and think about the fabric of time? I mean, it's like life's just a big loom, weaving us all together, you know? Way far out, bro. Pass me some more of that incense, will you?

◦ CARE AND HANDLING
Anoint me with patchouli, brother.

◉ IDEAL LOCATION IN HOME
Location is just a state of mind, man.

PISCES

Woven Tapestry

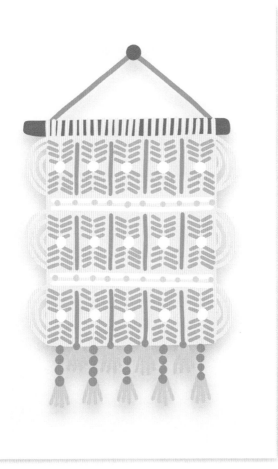

Carved Wooden Mask

The artisans who carved me were thinking religious ceremony, cultural celebration, or rite of passage, but I'd totally rather be part of your weirdo white-boy dance parties. Nice stanky leg. I'd poke my eyes out, but luckily someone did that for me.

🝑 **CARE AND HANDLING**
I'm a work of art—stop pretending I'm your girlfriend.

📍 **IDEAL LOCATION IN HOME**
Hang me where I can scare the living daylights out of small children.

SCORPIO

Maybe today this birdbrain will figure out that she needs to sit on me. I am, however, a bit concerned about the size of that featherless fanny. And this whole "which came first" thing is really scrambling my yolk. Holy egg-sistential crisis, Batman!

🌢 **CARE AND HANDLING**
Roost on me, draped in your red-feather boa. Clucking appreciated.

📍 **IDEAL LOCATION IN HOME**
Can we spoon in your queen-sized nest?

CANCER

Hand-Painted Egg

Tibetan Singing Bowl

MMMMMMmmmmm.
You are being soothed
by my healing vibrations.
MMMMmmmm. Your
essence is expanding.
MMMMMMmmmmmnnnn.
Your soul is soaring with
the song of the universe.
MMMMMmmmm. Fill me
with whipped cream and tickle
my bottom. *MMMMMmmm.*
What?—I have needs, too.

🌢 **CARE AND HANDLING**
Rub my rim and let the magic happen.

📍 **IDEAL LOCATION IN HOME**
Anywhere in the house is good, but my
bowl is for prayers, not toenail clippings.

LIBRA

Oh no, here we go again.
On goes the linen tunic. Nice britches, dude. Authentic.
If I have to be ferried around another RenFest in a scabbard while you greet people with "Good morrow" and stuff yourself with turkey legs, I'm gonna figure out how to stab myself.

◆ **CARE AND HANDLING**
Yikes, Lancelot, be careful!

♥ **IDEAL LOCATION IN HOME**
Yep, up on the wall above the bed, stud muffin. You are so tough. All the ladies know how tough you are.

ARIES

Decorative Sword

Ceramic Urn

Last night I had a beautiful
dream about being full
to the brim with human ashes.
Nighty, night! Sleep tight,
knowing that one day soon,
all that's left of *you* will fit
perfectly inside of *me*!

🖤 **CARE AND HANDLING**

Caress me with eulogies and prayers,
please. Or the mini-vac. Whatever.

📍 **IDEAL LOCATION IN HOME**

Oh, I don't know. Hypothetical question:
Where do you envision your charred
remains?

SCORPIO

SPIRITUAL
AND
MYSTICAL

Prepare to have your chakras aligned and your aura cleansed by these transcendental tchotchkes. They may look serene and enlightened, but don't be fooled by their lofty exteriors— there's nothing holy about what's going on in their metaphysical minds.

I've got some fortune and prosperity for you right here, my friend. I'll start by sharing the wealth of these luscious moobs and this nice round snuggle-drum. You're welcome.

💧 **CARE AND HANDLING**
Rub my belly and feed me Butterfingers.

📍 **IDEAL LOCATION IN HOME**
Where would you like blessings bestowed, my little kumquat?

TAURUS

Jade Laughing Buddha

Worry Stone

Global pandemic? Be gone.
Climate change? No problem.
Polarization, authoritarianism,
human rights abuses? On it.
Habitat loss, mass extinctions,
coral bleaching, and endangered
orangutans? Make it stop!
I'm just a rock. A rock! Quit
rubbing me and go write your
congressperson!

◊ **CARE AND HANDLING**
A little tenderness, please. I'm only hard on
the outside.

♦ **IDEAL LOCATION IN HOME**
Deep in the pocket of your old
green jacket. You never wear that
anymore? I had no idea.

ROCK

Slapping a crystal in the corner and hoping for a new life doesn't cut it. The energy around here is stagnant. We're talking toxic cosmic sludge. Do they make hazmat suits in my size?

CARE AND HANDLING
Bathe me in sunlight until my aura sparkles like a goddamn diamond. I need to be fully charged to take on this train wreck.

IDEAL LOCATION IN HOME
Where I can best feng your shui. Seriously, bring your shui over here so I can feng it.

AQUARIUS

Feng Shui Crystal

Dream Catcher

I signed up to protect sleepers from nightmares and evil spirits—a noble purpose steeped in tradition. But dear lord, the stuff that happens in that bed . . . Let's just say I've seen some things the ancestors never prepared me for. And don't blame me for those dreams about sentient mannequins. That's above my pay grade.

🌢 **CARE AND HANDLING**
Maybe shake me out a bit? I'm here to catch dreams, not dandruff.

📍 **IDEAL LOCATION IN HOME**
Kid's room, please. Bring on the monsters and boogeymen!

SCORPIO

Oy vey, this schmuck thinks I'm just a fancy candleholder. May curses rain down upon you! May you grow like an onion, with your head in the ground and your feet in the air! May all your teeth fall out, except one, so you can still have a toothache! May you find no rest, even in the grave!

◗ CARE AND HANDLING

Fill my branches with holy oil from trees grown on the Mount of Olives, just a day's worth, and watch me burn for eight! Or cram in cheap candles from your big box store's Hanukkah display. That works, too. Way to honor your ancestors, nudnik.

♥ IDEAL LOCATION IN HOME

Go ahead. Stick me next to the antique cross you're using as a jewelry rack.

DAVID

Menorah

Geode

I don't mean to be insensitive—
truly, I don't. OK, fine. I'm
insensitive. Pure crystal and
stone, formed in the heart of the
Earth. You, on the other hand, are
dandelion fluff. A wisp of cosmic
dust. Pull it together or hurl me
into the nearest volcano.

🌢 **CARE AND HANDLING**

My existence is a tribute to the Earth's
most powerful forces—pressure, time, and
transformation. Do your worst, buttercup.

📍 **IDEAL LOCATION IN HOME**

I was forged over millennia in the searing
heat of molten lava. Must I compete for
space on the mantel with snow globes
from the dollar store?

ROCK

USERNAME: NaughtyCherub#69

ABOUT ME: I'm ready to spread my wings and fly into thrilling new experiences. Interested in role-playing, power dynamics, and sensual domination. Let me feed your God complex and guide you through the gates of pleasure and pain. Discretion appreciated.

🜄 CARE AND HANDLING
Cleanse me with holy water while you serenade me with golden harps.

📍 IDEAL LOCATION IN HOME
Hang me next to the Velvet Elvis.
Talk about a hunka hunka burning love.

SCORPIO

Angel Ornament

Prayer Beads

Pick me up. Let's pray about it.
Sure, it's dramatic to be draped
over coffee-table books and
abstract metal sculptures,
but I'm here to save your soul,
not win you a design award.

🌢 **CARE AND HANDLING**
A little care and a little handling!

📍 **IDEAL LOCATION IN HOME**
Somewhere with soul. Or has soul gone out
of style, too?

VIRGO

What did I do to end up in this weed patch you call a garden? Bad karma from stepping on that spider? The time I took two mints from the candy bowl? My impure thoughts about Padma? I'll do better in this incarnation. I will only think loving thoughts about the dumbass who placed me here. Dipshit! Wait. Dammit! Next life.

🖤 **CARE AND HANDLING**
Circle me clockwise and place lotus blossoms on my toes.

📍 **IDEAL LOCATION IN HOME**
Under the Bodhi tree, facing east. Ok, under that scraggly maple you haven't managed to kill.

TAURUS

Golden Meditating Buddha

Crystal Ball

Will you get the long-deserved promotion? *Reply hazy, try again.* Will the hot guy at the gym ask you out? *Outlook not so good.* Get back into those skinny jeans? *Ask again later.* Win the lottery? *My sources say no.* Oh, come on, honey, give the soothsayers a shot! Try asking about nights in with Netflix and threadbare jammies. *Signs point to yes.*

🌢 **CARE AND HANDLING**
A nice dose of moonlight.

📍 **IDEAL LOCATION IN HOME**
Eye level. Gaze into my mysterious depths. Be awestruck.

SAGITTARIUS

FUNCTIONAL
AND
DECORATIVE

Who says practicality can't have personality? These tchotchkes have a purpose and serve up some attitude along with it. Don't be fooled by their functional facades—there just might be a world of dysfunction buried beneath.

MRS. SALT: Fine, I'll say it. You're lazy! Do I have to do everything around here? The only thing you do these days is make me sneeze.

MR. PEPPER: It's not my fault you're out there all day shaking your stuff for everyone. The delicate tastebuds these days can't appreciate a real man. Once upon a time we were the dream team. Remember our vow to keep things spicy together forever?

🌢 **CARE AND HANDLING**
Take your hands off Mrs. Salt for once! We know all about your sky-high blood pressure.

📍 **IDEAL LOCATION IN HOME**
Side by side. We may be dysfunctional, but we're committed.

GEMINI

Novelty Salt and Pepper Shakers

Brass Bell

Ding my dong.
Dingle my dangler.
You know you want to.

💧 **CARE AND HANDLING**
Ring my bell, baby.

📍 **IDEAL LOCATION IN HOME**
Hang me high where my brass ball
can swing.

LEO

I just want to hold down some paper. You know, that thin white stuff you write on? No? They use it to make books. You know, books? Still confused? Go ahead, keep on scrolling. Everything's just fine.

🖤 **CARE AND HANDLING**
Who cares? I'm obsolete.

📍 **IDEAL LOCATION IN HOME**
A desk would be nice, but the TV tray next to the couch works, too. We can binge-watch *The Office*.

TAURUS

Paperweight

Handmade Quilt

Granny Bea hummed ever-so-lovingly while she quilted me. Oh, the stories I heard about her precious pumpkin and how I would keep her nice and cozy. I was woefully unprepared for what that "sweet child" would be up to in the college dorms. Heavens to Betsy. My darling daisies had to cover their innocent eyes.

🌢 **CARE AND HANDLING**
Just don't turn me into a vest. I've seen the online videos.

📍 **IDEAL LOCATION IN HOME**
Folded on a rocker, dearie. No more beds for me. I'm too old for that nonsense.

CANCER

Ethereal beauties, we floated on a breeze until you impaled us to display our corpses. Seriously, who does that? That's some *Silence of the Lambs* level bullshit. Sleep with one eye open—Satan's coming for your soul.

🖤 **CARE AND HANDLING**
Call 911!!!

📍 **IDEAL LOCATION IN HOME**
There's no place for a monstrosity like me. You, however, belong in the seventh circle of Hell.

AQUARIUS

100

Butterfly Collection

Handmade
Pottery Bowl

Just because I was made in a beginner's night class at the community college doesn't mean I'm not a real bowl. I belong! I'm round enough, I'm stable enough, and doggone it, people like me!

CARE AND HANDLING
No soup, please. I'm a bit wobbly.

IDEAL LOCATION IN HOME
Oh, I don't know. A kitchen shelf is fine. The mantel is for the perfect porcelain.

CANCER

Phi Kappa Phelta Lota Delta's Micro Peenie! Chug, chug, chug!

💧 **CARE AND HANDLING**

Bro, do you even lift? ⅓ vodka, ⅔ protein powder. You'll thank me later.

📍 **IDEAL LOCATION IN HOME**

Next to the beer pong table, bruh! You got rid of it? Major buzzkill, dude.

DRUNK

Beer Stein

Metal Candleholder

Light me up to add a touch of romance. It's not like I'm obsessively imagining flames climbing the walls. No unbearable tension or compulsive thoughts about fiery chaos here. I keep dreaming about matches. I just need one little spark . . .

🕯 **CARE AND HANDLING**
Come on, baby, light my fire.

📍 **IDEAL LOCATION IN HOME**
Somewhere that needs mood lighting. Maybe under the curtains? Near the newspaper? In a puddle of gasoline?

ARIES

OMG. Books are, like, so cool. I totally read so many books. What was that one about the big whale? Like, Dick-something? It was so deep. Made me think, you know? Like, that one sailor guy who did all those things, that was, like, so inspiring. I'm totally inspired.

🌢 **CARE AND HANDLING**
Oh my god, gross, is that dust?!
Get it off me. Get it off!

📍 **IDEAL LOCATION IN HOME**
This is, like, confusing. Aren't books supposed to be all smart and stuff? Why can't they just stand up by themselves?

GEMINI

Brass Bookends

Ornate Mirror

Repeat after me: *You are smart. You are loved. You are beautiful.* Just kidding. You look like shit, and no one likes you.

CARE AND HANDLING
Be careful. I'm fragile, like your ego.

IDEAL LOCATION IN HOME
A bit higher, please. Even higher. That's right. Up where I can't see those jiggly bits.

VIRGO

I'm all for cleansing the air with my negative ions, but let's get some deodorant involved as well. The kind with chemicals, please. My powers only go so far with your "natural musk."

🖤 **CARE AND HANDLING**
Stop licking me, hippy. Eat a taco.

📍 **IDEAL LOCATION IN HOME**
A well-ventilated room, please.

TAURUS

Himalayan Salt Lamp

Participation Trophy

Oh, hell no! She didn't make a single goal all season! I swear she spent whole games rolling around on the grass or looking for ladybugs. Are we ok with this?! Is this what I got all shiny for? We're really setting up this "winner" for a lifetime of success here.

🌢 **CARE AND HANDLING**
Just let the tears of disappointment rain down on me when she discovers this is all a scam.

📍 **IDEAL LOCATION IN HOME**
Next to the framed diplomas you bought at Thrifty Bargain.

CAPRICORN

Cuckoo-cuckoo! Hah-loo! Hi! Look at me, am I not a pretty little birdie? Oh no, back in my chalet. Almost caught your eye that time. Halloo! Halloo! I'm back! Did you miss me?! Cuckoo-cuckoo! Uh oh, you're meditating? Baby asleep? So sorry, so sorry! Cuckoo-cuckoo! Halloo! I li again! Aren't I adorable? Don't you love me? I love you. Cuckoo-cuckoo! I love you! Cuckoo-cuckoo!

♦ **CARE AND HANDLING**
Stuff my little beak with Cocoa Puffs. I'm cuckoo for those things!

♥ **IDEAL LOCATION IN HOME**
Entryway, where I can greet your guests. Cuckoo-Cuckoo! Halloo!

GEMINI

Cuckoo Clock

Miniature Globe

Ok, but *prove* I'm round. You're so woke you can't see straight, and what you think is curvature is an illusion created by propaganda and ignorance. If I'm so "round," how am I not rolling off the shelf? Open your eyes, sheeple.

🌢 **CARE AND HANDLING**
You can't handle the truth, snowflake.

📍 **IDEAL LOCATION IN HOME**
Flat surface. Unless the government convinced you the shelf is round, too.

LEO

Library of Congress Cataloging-in-Publication Data available.

ISBN: 978-1-68555-621-1
Ebook ISBN: 978-1-68555-143-8
LCCN: 2024941397

Printed using Forest Stewardship Council® certified stock
from sustainably managed forests.

Manufactured in China.

Original Design by AJ Hansen.
Typesetting by Rachel Lopez Metzger.
Illustrations by Shutterstock.

1 3 5 7 9 10 8 6 4 2

The Collective Book Studio®
Oakland, California
www.thecollectivebook.studio

A tchotchke (CHOTCH-kee) is a knickknack, collectible, or miscellaneous item that decorates (or clutters) your shelves. The term has long been a favorite among Jewish Americans and has made its way into the quirky vernacular of New York City and beyond. Borrowed from Yiddish and of Slavic origin, the word *tchotchke* has a history as varied and colorful as the objects themselves. And, as we now know, these trinkets possess little minds that are just as fucked up as yours . . .

CONTENTS

Whimsical

Vintage and Collectibles

TCHOTCHKES

AND THEIR

F*CKED-UP

THOUGHTS

THE MESSED-UP MINDS OF
YOUR TRINKETS AND TREASURES

ELISABETH SAAKE

THE
collective
BOOK STUDIO

Cultural and Artisanal

Spiritual and Mystical

Functional and Decorative